A souvenir guide

Quebec House

Kent

The V
and V

A Hou

❧ National Trust

The Wolfe Family and Westerham

'We come to Westerham ... this is a handsome well-built market town, and is full of gentry, and consequently of good company.'

Daniel Defoe, 1724

Below The front of the house through the gate

Opposite The stained-glass window memorial to James Wolfe in Westerham Church, after Edward Burne-Jones (1833–98) in 1909

Defoe visited Westerham shortly before Edward Wolfe and his much younger bride moved to the town. The 39-year-old, half-pay lieutenant-colonel and his wife, 22-year-old Henrietta, rented Quebec House, then called Spiers, from the town's steward, Thomas Ellis.

Ellis lived nearby at Well Street, later to become Chartwell and the home of Winston Churchill. Despite the centuries dividing them, Wolfe and Churchill lived in Westerham for similar reasons. The combination of glorious countryside, good company and just a 22-mile journey to London still brings people to live in Westerham today.

A family affair

News of the Wolfe's arrival stirred much interest amongst the townsfolk, and soon the pretty Yorkshire woman made friends with long-established local families. Just six months later, whilst Edward was away on military duty, Henrietta gave birth to the first of two sons; James Wolfe was born on 2 January 1727. Almost exactly a year later a second son, Edward, arrived.

Fit to fight

The boys grew up in the town and James became life-long friends with George Warde whose family purchased Squerryes Court in 1731; his descendants still live there today.

James was destined to be a soldier. Only poor health prevented him from joining his father's regiment on the expedition to Cartagena, when he was just 13 years old. A little over a year later, in the gardens at nearby Squerryes Court, he received news of his first commission. The Warde family and the people of Westerham have long been proud of their association with James Wolfe.

'… a middle aged Colonel, late married to a young and pretty Yorkshire woman, Miss Thompson …'

An extract from Mary Lewis's letter to her sister, 3 July 1726

A House of Intrigue

'I can now picture Wolfe not upon the silent St Lawrence in the darkness of the night, but as a delicate, pale little boy in the silence and the darkness of that old house.'

H.V. Morton, 1942

Quebec House with its twelve gables, mellow Kentish ragstone and soft brickwork is pleasing to look at and appears, at first glance, to be of one homogeneous build. However, closer inspection reveals a hidden history: this is a house that wears the scars of alteration with great style.

Early beginnings

Long known as the Parish Meade, documentary evidence has revealed that there was a building on this land as early as the thirteenth or fourteenth centuries. However, no traces of this can be found either on site or in the archives. Internal windows, blocked doorways, stone fireplaces and the surviving timber frame provide enough evidence for us to reconstruct the house that must have stood on this site since the 1530s. Tantalisingly, the overmantel in the Parlour bears the crest of Henry VII that hints at an earlier date.

In the 1630s this L-shaped Tudor house was extensively remodelled to form an almost square double-pile house that was known as Spiers. By the end of the Georgian period the front of the house had a square façade with blind windows and parapet wall, and it was renamed Quebec House in memory of its most famous resident.

Above **Re-enactment scene in the Drawing Room**

Left **The overmantel in the Parlour**

Opposite **The Parlour window was blocked in the 1630s**

Mid-sixteenth century

1730s

End ninteenth century

Splendour to squalor

During the nineteenth century the owners of the house fell on hard times and the property fell into disrepair. In April 1839, William Howard wrote in a letter to his brother John (who later purchased the property):

'I am sorry to see Quebec House and premises so neglected. The house is covered with dirt and rubbish and the garden totally neglected and nothing planted in it this spring. Surely it would be better if Mr. Gautrell would allow someone to clean out the house and garden. It is not fit to [rent out] soon.'

Most of the two-acre garden was sold for development and by 1849 the house had been divided in two. Quebec House east continued as a family home whilst Quebec House west was occasionally used as accommodation. It also became a school and later a doctor's surgery.

The historian Arthur Bradley wrote in 1895 that 'Quebec House suggests infinite possibilities for the hand of some reverent restorer'. In 1900, a restorer was found; Charles Warde bought the house and reunited it into a single residence. Soon he employed the county architect, Granville Streatfield, and they set about ensuring the house was returned to its original appearance at the time the Wolfe family lived here.

A Canadian journalist and author, Beckles Willson, tenanted Quebec House in 1907. Whilst here he transcribed Wolfe's letters and wrote the definitive work *Wolfe's Life and Letters*. In 1912 Charles Warde died and his estate offered the house for sale. Rumours in both British and Canadian press reported that a rich American planned to buy the House and transport it to the USA.

A lasting legacy

Beckles Willson started a campaign amongst his contacts to save Quebec House. Joseph Learmont, a wealthy Montreal businessman and philanthropist, had a great interest in early Canadian history and when he received news of the threat to the house he decided to buy it for the Canadian nation. Sadly he died before the gift could be finalised. His widow, Charlotte, was determined to see his wishes fulfilled.

Thanks to the intervention of another Canadian, Sir Campbell Stuart, early in 1917 the house was given to the National Trust. Although the National Trust owned other buildings at this time, Quebec House was the first gift of a house and collection.

A welcome retreat

Amongst the first visitors to the house was the staff of the Ottawa War Hospital, which had opened in Orpington to treat Canadian soldiers wounded during the First World War. The upper floors were used as a bandage factory during this time. It seems appropriate that soon after the medical staff visited, wounded Canadian soldiers also came to the house.

The first visitors to Quebec House saw only the three front rooms on the ground floor. The late seventeenth-century Dining Room was restored and opened to visitors as the Bicentenary Room to mark the 200th anniversary of Wolfe's death in 1959. The Drawing Room on the first floor was opened in the 1980s whilst the project to decorate the Bedroom as it had been in Wolfe's time and

open it to the public was conceived to mark the 250th anniversary of his death in 2009. Over the coming years we plan to open more of the house to visitors to give a real sense of the family home that James Wolfe would have known.

Top During the First World War, Quebec House was commissioned as a bandage factory

Above Canadian soldiers visited Quebec House during the First World War

Right An 'At Home' invitation to wounded soldiers

Mr. & Mrs. Wolfe-Aylward

At Home

To Wounded Soldiers from

Dunsdale Hospital.

Quebec House,
Once the Home of Major-General
James Wolfe.

Westerham.

Thursday,
Dec. 21, 1916.

is well cared for, the building is fragile. Traces of the Tudor timber frame are buried in the walls of the house, only part of the building has foundations and it is built on a sandy river bed; glance at the rear wall of the house and you can see the effects of many years of structural movement. We manage the building by careful monitoring and through regular maintenance. The support you give us by buying this guidebook, visiting the house and donating to our conservation projects allows this vital work to continue.

Left The water pump bears the date 1792

Below A commemorative plaque records Joseph Learmont's admiration for General Wolfe

A fragile fortune

The Learmonts set a difficult task when they gave the house to the National Trust. Their desire was that the house be furnished as it might have been when Wolfe lived here, it should tell the story of Wolfe's life and death as well as be a place that celebrates early Canadian history. How can you tell the story of a soldier's life and death in a house furnished as it would have been when he lived there if he was just a boy then?

Over the years we have interpreted this task in different ways, opening more rooms to give additional sense of that childhood home. Today with the exhibition in the Coach House and more rooms open than ever before we are able to tell the story of Wolfe's life, show how some rooms might have looked when he lived here and tell his story alongside the history of the house itself.

Charlotte Learmont ensured we had the funds to build the collection you see today. An important part of our work here is to ensure that it is fully understood and that we continue to enhance it. In recent years we have added to our maps and received donations of several important artefacts to the collection.

At the heart of the National Trust is conservation, and at Quebec House this is especially difficult. Although the collection

JOSEPH BOWLES LEARMONT
OF MONTREAL CANADA
BORN MAY 15TH 1839 DIED MARCH 12TH 1914
FOR THE LOVE AND ADMIRATION OF
WOLFE
HE BOVGHT THIS HOVSE AND
BEQVEATHED IT TO THE NATION

Born to be a Soldier

'... the battle James Wolfe fought ... altered the world in a dramatic and lasting way.'

'Death or Victory, The Battle of Quebec and the Birth of an Empire', 2009, Dan Snow

The siege

Wolfe's fame grew from his great victory at Quebec, securing North America from the French. This victory came at the end of a savage and uncertain campaign. The bulk of his forces left Britain in February 1759. The 49 warships, 117 merchant ships, with 2,100 marines and 9,160 soldiers made up his army. More troops from the colonies joined the army in Nova Scotia. With his forces assembled, Wolfe's invasion fleet entered the St Lawrence River.

The Royal Navy's successful navigation of the dangerous and uncharted river allowed Wolfe's army to land close to the city. The French had depended on river pilots to navigate each section of the river. Wolfe had the gifted surveyor Samuel Holland and the young navigator James Cook amongst his numbers. They were able to guide the British ships through the treacherous traverse of the St Lawrence. Quebec's first line of defence had been beaten.

Attack!

On 27 June the army began to land unopposed on the Ile d'Orleans. The most dangerous time during any amphibious operation is when the troops are still afloat. The day after the British began to land, the French tried to destroy the soldiers on the river by attacking with fire ships. They were no threat. In small boats British sailors rowed up-wind of the flames and used grappling hooks to tow the French fire boats away.

By 12 July Wolfe had established camps, hospitals and artillery batteries along the river. No relief for the defenders would come from the water. The bombardment of the city could begin.

Left *The Taking of Quebec*, after Hervey Garrett Smith

A desperate attempt

In broad daylight at 8am on 31 July Wolfe led his men to assault the French positions below Quebec at Montmorency. The assault was a disaster. Mud prevented the boats from reaching the shore and those men who did reach the river bank rushed ahead to the French entrenchments – they were easily repulsed. Only the rain saved Wolfe's army, which suffered 440 casualties and gained nothing.

After the defeat at Monmorency the siege took a savage turn. Soldiers on both sides committed atrocities, and scalping was commonplace. Wolfe adopted a strategy of attrition: 'upward of 1,400 of their farm houses' were burnt and many rural communities were destroyed in his attempts to starve the city into surrender.

The British had arrived with 163 cannons and 75,000 cannon balls. After the siege, in the lower town alone, 535 houses had been burnt down. The oldest city in North America lay in ruins.

Frustration with progress led many to despair that the city would ever fall; even Wolfe doubted he would succeed.

In his final dispatch to Pitt, written on 2 September, the young general began to contemplate the failure of his mission.

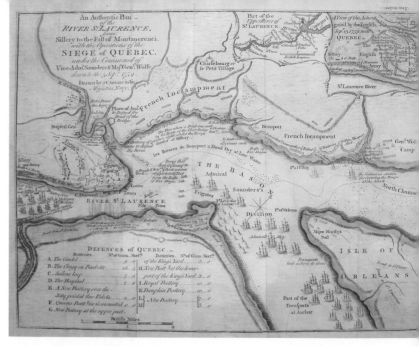

On 9 September Wolfe led a reconnaissance and from Gorham's Point spotted a difficult path that followed the Anse au Foulon from the river to the Plains of Abraham. He planned to cross the river, land his troops just before dawn above the city and take the French by surprise. Some 3,600 men were about to climb to their place in history; the battle for Quebec was about to begin.

Above A plan of the St Lawrence River showing the operations of the Siege of Quebec, under the command of Vice Admiral Saunders and Major General Wolfe, up to 5 September 1759

Below left *Vue De Québec* 1755, by Georges Louis Le Rouge

Below Cannonballs on display in the Bicentenary Room

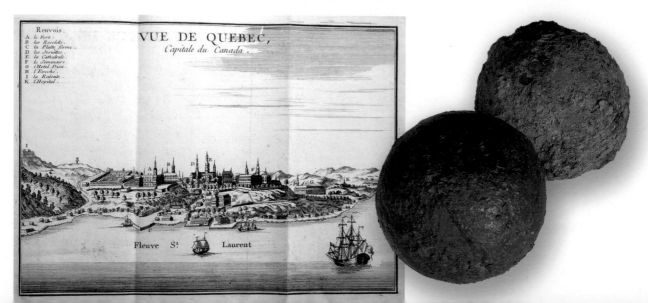

The Battle of Quebec

12 September
Late evening

The largest battleships of the fleet make a demonstration off the French camp at Beaufort near Montmorency. The French commander, Marquis de Montcalm, is unsure; will the British try to assault here again? Could this be the main British assault? What about the troops who have moved above the city?

13 September
4am

Wolfe's light infantry drift too far downstream and land above the Anse au Foulon. They scale the 180ft cliffs. The few French defenders are taken by surprise and flee to the city. The landing site is left undefended. Over the coming hours Wolfe is able to land 3,600 of his best troops and they climb the steep track to the Plains of Abraham. Soon his army is deployed in battle formation above Quebec city.

7am

News of the landings at Foulon begins to reach Montcalm. Uncertain that this is the main assault he does not react immediately.

10am

The French troops arrive on the Plains of Abraham. Aware how desperate his position is, Montcalm orders an immediate assault in three broad columns. The tactics of his different types of troops and the uneven ground mean the columns quickly break up and become a rabble. The French advance and fire. The British stay in their thin red line and hold fire. The French advance further and fire once again. Still the British hold firm. When the French are within 40 paces the British line fires. Wolfe's belief in training and his ability to discipline an army to the Prussian drill pays off. After just one more rippling volley, the fighting lasts less than 15 minutes, the French are defeated and flee the plains. General Wolfe is wounded three times during the battle. Knowing that news of his injuries will affect the men, he asks to be taken quietly from the battlefield. Realising the extent of his wounds, he refuses a surgeon: 'it is all over with me'. He lives just long enough to know that the French have fled. He gives one last order to cut off their retreat and utters his final words 'Now, God be praised, I will die in peace'. Beaten, disorganised and demoralised, the French troops retreat to their camp at Beaufort and into the city. The militia and other local troops make a last stand which stops the British from cutting off their retreat. Montcalm is wounded during the battle when a cannonball knocked him from his horse. Mortally wounded he is taken into the city but dies the next day. The bulk of the French army escapes towards Montreal: they will return to fight another day. The city is in ruins and with most of its defenders retreating they have little choice.

18 September

The city surrenders to the British Army.

Who was General Wolfe?

Domestic Life

February 1724
Edward Wolfe marries Henrietta Thompson at Long Marston, York

Summer 1726
They move to Westerham and rent Spiers

2 January 1727
First son, James, born at the vicarage

28 January 1729
Second son, Edward, born

1731
Warde family buy Squerryes Court; George Warde, aged 14, becomes friends with both boys

General James Wolfe as a Young Man, after Joseph Highmore (1692–1780)

1738
The family move to Greenwich and the boys both go to the school run by the Revd. Swinden

September 1744
Younger brother Edward falls sick whilst serving with the army in Flanders and dies of consumption

Elizabeth Lawson

January 1748
On leave in London, courts Elizabeth Lawson, maid of honour to the Princess of Wales

December 1748
Parents against friendship with Elizabeth, would rather he marries Miss Hoskins from Croydon

March 1749
While in Glasgow studies Latin and maths in his spare time, seeks leave to complete his education

November 1750
Parents still want James to marry Miss Hoskins despite his intention to marry Elizabeth

February 1751
Miss Hoskins marries John Warde

Early 1751
Falls out with parents and is rejected by Elizabeth

1724–1737   1738–1743   1743–1746   1746–1748   1749–1751

Military Career

James's father, *Edward Wolfe,* attributed to Sir James Thornhill (1675–1734)

July 1740
Intends to join his father in an expedition to Cartagena but falls sick and is sent home to Greenwich

3 November 1741
Commissioned 2nd Lieutenant in his father's regiment

February 1743
Younger brother, Edward, commissioned into same regiment as James

27 June 1743
James distinguishes himself at the Battle of Dettingen; his horse is shot from under him and his good conduct is noted by the Duke of Cumberland

July 1743
Appointed Adjutant and Lieutenant in the 12th Foot

June 1744
Promoted Captain in 4th Foot

12 June 1745
Appointed Brigade-Major to Pulteney's Brigade

September 1745
His regiment returns from Flanders to deal with Jacobite uprising

17 January 1746
Takes part in Battle of Falkirk, his regiment is one of the few that retreats in good order; James appointed aide-de-camp to General Hawley

April 1746
Sees action at the Battle of Culloden which ends the Highland uprising

2 July 1747
Wounded at the Battle of Lauffeld; receives thanks from Duke of Cumberland for his gallant behaviour

The Battle of Lauffeld, July 1747, by Pierre L'Enfant (1704–87)

January 1749
Appointed major in 20th Foot and begins compiling his Instructions for Young Officers

March 1750
Aged 23, James is promoted to Lieutenant Colonel 20th Foot; applies for special leave to undertake military studies abroad

June–August 1752
Spends time in Ireland: visits his paternal uncle, Major Walter Wolfe

Autumn 1752
Travels to Europe and spends six months in Paris completing his education; visits the French court at Versailles and is presented to Louis XV and Madame Pompadour

Summer 1754
On leave at Blackheath he visits Sir John Mordaunt and the Wardes at Westerham

The miniature portrait of *Miss Katherine Lowther* worn in a locket by Wolfe up to the very day before his death

December 1758
James becomes 'unofficially' engaged to Katherine Lowther. Makes his last visit to Westerham

January 1759
James given command of expedition to capture Quebec by Pitt

February 1759
Visits parents in Bath before sailing for North America on 17th

26 March 1759
Edward Wolfe dies aged 72. James wears a black armband during the Battle of Quebec in memory of his father

Henrietta Wolfe, by an unknown British artist

17 October 1759
News of James's death reaches his mother

20 November 1759
James buried in the family vault with his father at St Alpheges, Greenwich

26 September 1764
Mother dies and is also buried in the family vault alongside her husband and elder son

Summer 1771
Benjamin West exhibits his *Death of General Wolfe* at the Royal Academy

November 1773
Wilton monument to Wolfe unveiled in Westminster Abbey

1752 –1756   *1757 –1758*   *1758 –1759*   *1759 –1763*   *1764 –1773*

Winter 1753-4
Stationed at Dover Castle preparing plans to prevent French landing in event of war

May 1756
Britain declares war on France

James in the uniform of the 20th foot

August 1757
Appointed quartermaster to expedition to Rochfort under Sir John Mordaunt

September 1757
Sails to reconnoitre French coast – recommends plan of action that is approved but no attack takes place

October 1757
Appointed colonel of 67th Foot

January 1758
Appointed one of three brigade commanders for expedition to Louisbourg

June 1758
Leads a successful landing against the French fortress and silences a battery leaving the harbour open for British attack

July 1758
Louisbourg captured

June 1759
Disembarks troops on the Isle d'Orleans

July 1759
Establishes batteries at Point Levis

31 July 1759
Abortive attempt to land at Montmorency Falls

Early September 1759
Falls ill and command passes to the brigadiers

9 September 1759
Recovers and leads reconnaissance on south side of river; begins to formulate plan

10 September 1759
Decides on surprise landing on north shore at Anse au Foulon

13 September 1759
4am British land; battle for Quebec on Plains of Abraham; James mortally wounded

17 October 1759
News of the victory at Quebec reaches Britain

1768
Wolfe's *Instructions to Young Officers* published

Medal commemorating the British victories of 1759

Tour of the House

The Entrance Hall

The panelling dates from the seventeenth century, but it was extensively patched after a flood in 1968. The Tudor fireplace contains a most appropriate Wealden cast-iron fireback, decorated with the French fleur-de-lys, which appears on the Province of Quebec's flag.

The set of nine watercolours by Edward Dayes illustrates the uniforms and arms drill of the Lancashire Militia in the late eighteenth century. Given to Quebec House by a descendant of Katherine Lowther, they display many of the drill movements Wolfe so successfully trained his men to carry out.

Above the fireplace hangs a flintlock musket of 1758. This was the standard firearm of the infantry soldier. The halberd in the corner was carried by a sergeant, more as a badge of rank than a weapon.

Left **The dresser in the Entrance Hall**

Above **Dressing-up clothes for visitors**

Opposite **The fireplace in the Entrance Hall with portraits of Mr and Mrs Joseph Bowles Learmont above**

The Parlour

A decorative graining has been applied to the seventeenth-century pine panelling, to match the finish in evidence during the Wolfes' occupancy. Above the fireplace is a carved overmantel with the much-mutilated arms of Henry VII inserted. In one corner is the Tudor window that was blocked when the staircase behind was added in the 1630s.

The maps and engravings in this room tell the story of why Quebec was so strategically important and help us to understand Wolfe's military career. The most impressive painting is that above the bureau by Richard Paton, *The Capture of Louisbourg, 1758,* in which Wolfe played such a prominent part.

The corner cabinet contains some of our most precious items: Henrietta's Wolfe's ring, the bonbonierre given to Wolfe by his fiancée Katherine Lowther, his snuff box, a miniature portrait of his aunt, Ann Burcher. Her descendants ensured many of these artefacts survived and passed them to the National Trust in the 1930s.

Above **The Parlour**

Left **The night soil cupboards in the Parlour**

Far left **A model of James Wolfe's landing craft**

The room is dominated by a bronze cast of the bust of Wolfe by Joseph Wilton (1722–1803). He is shown attired in classical garb, with the rather nice touch of epaulettes in the shape of wolf heads. Unfortunately, decay prevented Wilton from taking a death mask of Wolfe's face, nor were there any lifetime portraits of him as a grown man. However, a servant of Lord Gower, who bore a striking resemblance to Wolfe, served as a model, with help from Lord Edgcumbe, who corrected the finer details from memory.

Left A view through the Parlour door

The Bicentenary Room

This room was added when the house was altered in the 1630s. Originally a great parlour, the family's principal dining room, in the nineteenth century it was divided and used as a kitchen and pantries. Fortunately, its bolection-moulded panelling, which dates from about 1680, was not removed. In 1959, to mark the bicentenary of the death of Wolfe and the capture of Quebec, it was restored to its former state. The room now houses some of the most important art and artefacts associated with General Wolfe.

The series of images depicting the *Death of General Wolfe* show the influence Benjamin West's painting had on the eighteenth-century art world; records of heroic death would never be the same again.

At the other end of the room is Wolfe's quilted cotton dressing gown, in which his body was wrapped for transport back to England. The telescope that once belonged to Col. Williamson, who commanded the Royal Artillery at Quebec, was used by Wolfe when he led the reconnaissance that

Previous page *The Capture of Louisbourg 1758*, by Richard Paton (1717–91)

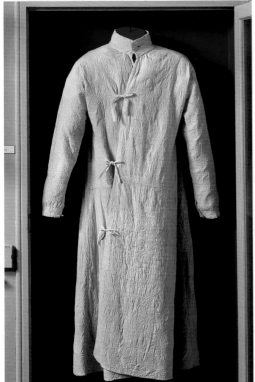

Travelling in style

The travelling canteen demonstrates the comfort in which an eighteenth-century general officer contrived to live while on active service; it was made for use during the Quebec campaign. After Wolfe's death it came into the possession of one of his brigadiers, the Hon. Robert Monckton, in whose family it descended to the 7th Viscount Galway, by whom it was presented to the United Services Institution and thence to the National Trust. A number of the original fitted contents are in the showcase nearby, including griddle, frying pan, canisters, cruet and glass decanters.

discovered the steep pathway leading to the Plains of Abraham.

The profile of Wolfe drawn by Hervey Smyth from life can be seen to the right of the fireplace. This sketch appears entirely spontaneous and was drawn on a page torn from a notebook shortly before the battle. It is close to being a caricature, emphasising Wolfe's distinctive features of sloping forehead, pointed nose and receding chin. The drawing has been the source for the many posthumous portraits of Wolfe, such as the full-length oil, after J.S.C. Schaak, which hangs nearby.

Above James Wolfe's dressing gown

The Inner Hall, Staircase and Landing

These spaces were also added when the house was altered in the 1630s. Recent dendrochronology shows that the five newel posts on the staircase were all from the same trunk, felled in around 1605. The use of Tuscan columns on the staircase is an important early example of English classicism.

The engravings that line the stairs are of Wolfe's contemporaries from the Quebec campaign. Ligonier was the commander-in-chief of the army and along with Pitt was responsible for Wolfe's appointment to lead the Quebec campaign.

The series of engravings of Quebec that rise to the first-floor landing was drawn by Richard Short who travelled with Wolfe's forces. These contemporary images give us a tremendous insight into how developed Quebec city was in 1759 but also the savage nature of the campaign. Many show evidence of the damage caused by the British siege. Some of the buildings can be recognised in Quebec city today.

The influence of West's painting is seen once again in the Toile du Jouy panel, a rare survival of this eighteenth-century type of printed fabric.

Right The Staircase
columns and banister

The Bedroom

The Bedroom is the final part of the 1630s additions to the house. The room was still in use by tenants as a bedroom until work to restore it to its appearance in the days of General Wolfe started in 2010.

Although the iron grate and bolection-moulded surround are old, they have only been here since the 1900 Warde restoration. Almost certainly they were brought in from Squerryes Court. The rest of the fireplace and the two closets are an important survival from the 1630s house. Paint analysis shows they were installed at that time as part of a very fashionable classical scheme; although repainted many times the colour scheme has been little altered.

The bed and cot in this room are modern replicas of eighteenth-century originals. The bed is based on George II's travelling bed whilst the cot is reminiscent of those found in conversation paintings of the eighteenth century. Both are indicative of the furniture owned by the Wolfe family.

The powder cloak was worn by General Wolfe to prevent wig whitener from damaging his clothes whilst dressing. Below sits the family bible and next to this is a copy of the Wolfe family tree, originally prepared in 1963 by the, Garter King of Arms and extended in 1986 by courtesy of the Wolfe Society. On its reverse side is another tree showing Wolfe's descent through his mother's side from Edward III and Hotspur.

Above **Artist's impression of the restored Bedroom**

Below **The newly restored fireplace in the Bedroom**

Below left **The Wolfe family Bible**

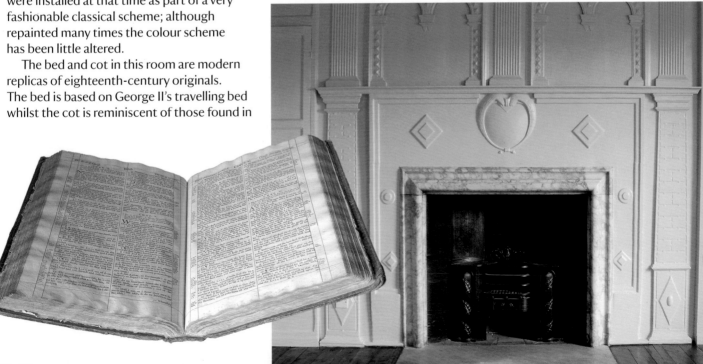

The Drawing Room

This large panelled room overlooking the front garden was restored to its original appearance during the extensive alterations carried out by Col. Charles Warde in 1900. The fireplace has a fine late seventeenth-century bolection-moulded surround of grey-veined marble, and the panelling is principally seventeenth-century.

Family portraits dominate the drawing room; the young James Wolfe hangs between his parents. The portrait of Edward, James's father, has long been associated with James Thornhill. It was discovered in a sale at the start of the twentieth century and was brought to Quebec House by Beckles Willson whilst he was tenant here. That of Henrietta is by an unknown artist and has been much altered. Careful examination shows details of several conservation and restoration campaigns.

The central image was believed to be an early twentieth-century copy of the original work by Joseph Highmore which is now in the Canadian National Gallery, Ottawa. The original was painted for the Rev. Swinden, Wolfe's tutor at Greenwich. A descendant of his donated this copy to Quebec House in the 1930s. Recent conservation work has revealed a very different history for this painting. The preparation of the canvas and style of painting demonstrate that it was made in the eighteenth century and we now believe it may be from Highmore's studio.

Opposite Writing equipment
for visitor activities in
the Drawing Room

In the corner next to the panelled door is an attractive late seventeenth-century longcase clock. The movement is by the well-known London clockmaker Edmund Aplee of Charing Cross, whose name is engraved on the dial. The walnut case, inlaid with marquetry, is contemporary with the movement, though the base is a later addition.

Between the windows is a William and Mary cushion-framed mirror, which has lost its cresting but retains its original softly bevelled plate. The leather wing armchair, dated to around 1760, has a particularly pleasing shape and still has much of its original leather covering.

On the Broadwood square piano is a framed piece of eighteenth-century music entitled *Britannia or the Death of Wolfe*, whose words reflect the sentimentality of the age. They were written by the author of *The Rights of Man*, Thomas Paine. He became editor of the *Pennsylvania Magazine*, in which he published the song in March 1775, commenting to the publishers that 'I have not pursued the worn out tract of modern song, but have thrown it into fable.'

Above left James's father, Edward Wolfe, attributed to Sir James Thornhill (1675–1734)

Above right Henrietta Wolfe, by an unknown artist

Below A Bow figurine of General Wolfe

The Garden and Coach House

When the family lived at Quebec House, the garden included the adjacent land that is now Westerham Place. Whilst we have no images of how the garden looked at that time, important documentary evidence survives in the form of Mrs Wolfe's recipe book. Her original book was inherited by George Warde and is on display at Squerryes Court.

Mrs Wolfe was an enthusiastic correspondent and collected recipes, many of which found their way into her 180-page notebook. These recipes give us a guide to the ingredients available nearby.

To boyl a carp ye french way
'Mix verjuice [an acid liquor expressed from crab apples or unripe grapes] and water with four onions, a bunch of sweet herbs, a little salt, cloves and peper. Put in ye belly of ye carp, half a ld of butter with some salt and cloves. When tis boyld put into ye liquor a pint of vinegar & let ye carp lye in it til tis almost cold. Serve to ye table dry and garnesh it with herbs.'

Below The view across the rear lawn to St Mary's Church

In 1792 Quebec House was renovated by its new owner, John Saunders. A new water source was dug in the garden and a water pump fitted. The Saunders family sold the house in 1846. By 1849 the new owners, the Howard family, were in financial trouble and they divided the house in two, Quebec House east and west, living in Quebec House east and letting Quebec House west for a number of uses over the years. The garden was also divided in half but a series of maps shows that the layout of the flowerbeds in the garden has remained largely unchanged since 1846. In 1900 the house was bought by the Warde family of Squerryes Court in a dilapidated state. Local tradition is that it was to become a working man's hostel. The Wardes could not bear this idea; they bought the house, reunited it as a single home and carefully restored it to its appearance at the time the Wolfe family lived here.

An engraving of the garden that belonged to Pendock Price, a house now known as Wolfelands at the west end of town, dates to the 1720s and helps us to understand the latest fashion for gardens in Westerham at that time. There is little possibility of ever recreating the garden as it would have been known to the Wolfe family, but by using the recipe book, the engraving and documentary evidence of plant species that were used in other gardens during the 1720s we are able to capture the essence of how their garden may have been.

Left Niche in the wall called a bee bole which houses the skep, or wicker basket, for bees

Below The spring border

Bottom The vegetable garden

The Coach House

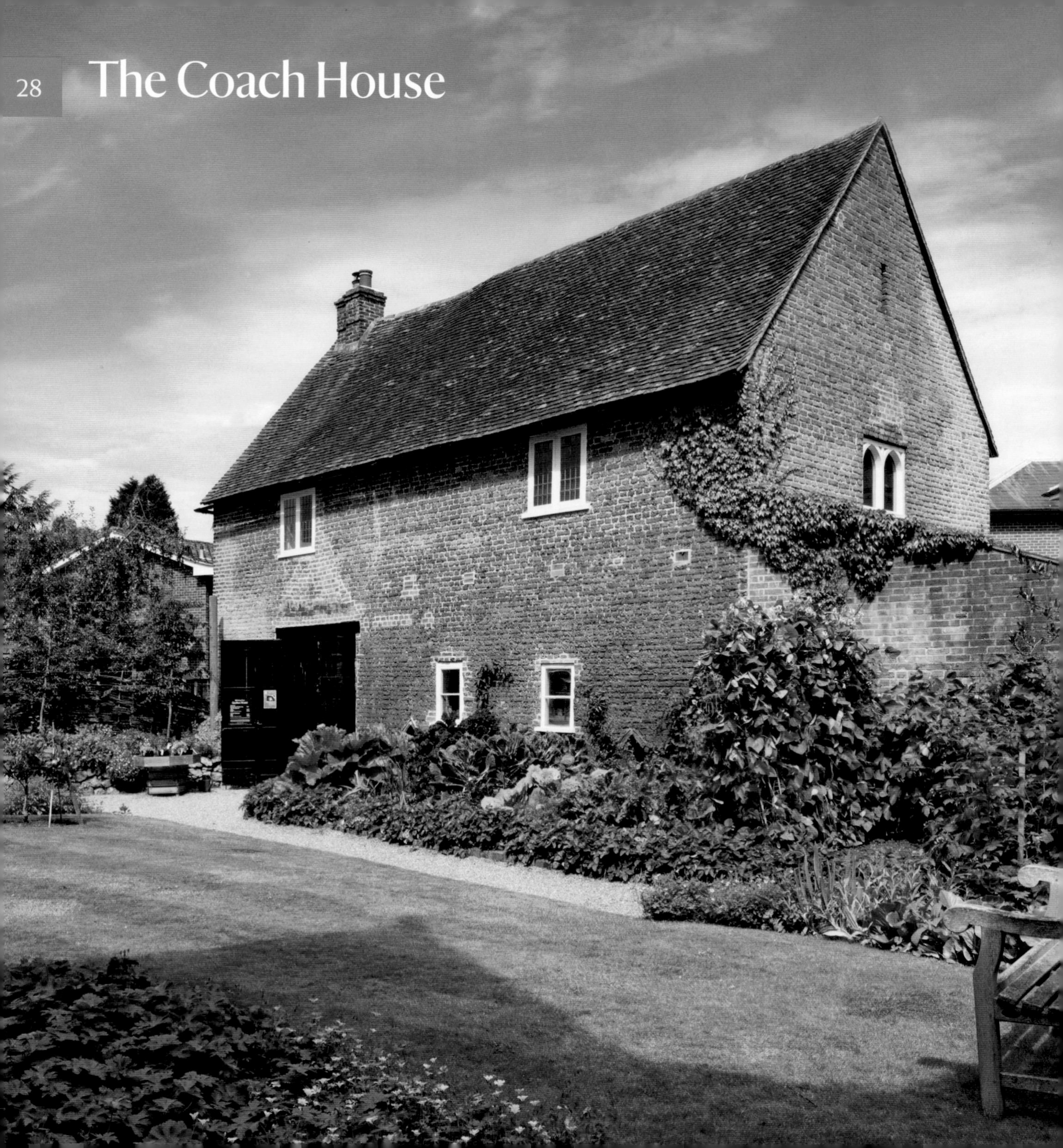

The Coach House is also an important building. Although it has changed over the years, its use has always echoed how people have lived in the main building. Originally built at the time the main house was altered in the 1630s, it was used as a barn with stables and a tack room on the ground floor and a hay loft on the first floor.

Reflecting changes in how the family used the main house and an increasing desire for privacy away from servants, the bread oven and open fireplace were added some time before 1700. The food for the family in the main house was prepared in this kitchen. A fireplace was also added to the first floor and an attic room where servants would have lived.

When the main house was divided in two, the building was also divided. The doors were added and it took the form we see today. Eventually the whole building was used for storage. In 2009 the National Trust completed conservation of the Coach House. The proximity of the building to the sandy bed of the River Darent had caused structural movement so the building was stabilised by underpinning the chimney and the installation of 130 steel pins.

Today the ground floor houses our visitor reception and coffee shop whilst upstairs an exhibition tells the story of General Wolfe's life from Westerham to Quebec.

The Coach House during the 1630s when it was a barn with stables and a tack room on the ground floor and a hay loft on the first floor

A bread oven and open fireplace were added to the kitchen before 1700 where food was prepared for the main house. A fireplace was added to the first floor and an attic room created for the servants

By 1880 when the house was divided, new doors to enable a coach to enter, were added

A Revolution in Art

On the eve of battle General Wolfe recited Thomas Gray's masterpiece, *Elegy Written in a Country Churchyard*. John Robison, a midshipman at the time, recalled Wolfe claiming he 'would rather have been the author of the poem than have the glory of beating the French the next day.'

Wolfe's death had a profound effect on the arts in the eighteenth century, and the cultural elite vied to immortalise his memory. Sermons were preached and published across Britain and North America, and Thackeray and Johnson dramatised Wolfe's life in their novels *The Virginians* and *Crystal*. Adam, Roubiliac, Cheere, Rysback, Carlini, Chambers and Tyler as well as Joseph Wilton, the leading sculptors of the day, competed for the commission to design a fitting memorial in Westminster Abbey.

Elegy Written in a Country Churchyard

The boast of heraldry, the pomp of power,
And all that beauty, all that wealth e'er gave,
Awaits alike the inevitable hour.
The paths of glory lead but to the grave.

Nor you, ye proud, impute to these the fault,
If Memory o'er their tomb no trophies raise,
Where through the long-drawn aisle and fretted vault
The pealing anthem swells the note of praise.

Can storied urn or animated bust
Back to its mansion call the fleeting breath?
Can Honour's voice provoke the silent dust,
Or Flattery soothe the dull cold ear of Death.

Thomas Gray, 1750

Benjamin West's *The Death of General Wolfe* was celebrated as a masterpiece of composition; the artist subtly merged overt classical references into a contemporary setting. The resultant work led Joshua Reynolds to announce,

'I foresee that this picture will not only become one of the most popular, but occasion a revolution in art.'

Eventually West sold five large and numerous smaller versions of his painting.

The engraving by William Wollett became the most popular selling image of the eighteenth century. Generations of artists were influenced by West's work; records of heroic death would never be the same again.

Edward Penny had made a painting of the *Death of General Wolfe* several years before West (see back cover); the original is now in the Ashmolean at Oxford. Penny didn't attempt a classical composition and also largely ignored the conventions of eighteenth-century history painting. Whilst his painting is much less famous and far less important to the history of art than West's image, the significance of Penny's painting is its historical accuracy. He has clearly been informed by actual accounts of Wolfe's death, since his image matches the research completed by Knox and published in 1761.

Stanzas

(On the taking of Quebec, and the death of General Wolfe)

Amidst the clamour of exulting joys,
Which triumph forces from the patriot heart;
Grief dares to mingle her soul-piercing voice,
And quells the raptures which from pleasures start.

O Wolfe! to thee a streaming flood of woe,
Sighing we pay, and think e'en conquest dear;
Quebec in vain shall teach our breast to glow,
Whilst thy sad fate extorts the heart-wrung tear.

Alive, the foe thy dreadful vigour fled,
And saw thee fall with joy-pronouncing eyes:
Yet they shall know thou conquerest, though dead!
Since from thy tomb a thousand heroes rise.

From *The Poetical Works of Oliver Goldsmith*, Wolfe's cousin, (1728–74). First printed in *The Busy Body*, 22 October 1759

Left *Monument to General James Wolfe,* by Joseph Wilton, 1772, in Westminster Abbey